Experiencing God

Experiencing God

Alan Ames

Layout and design:
Andreas Zureich – Germany.

ISBN 978-0-9820329-5-4

In memory of W.H. Bott

Contents

Preface

In these writings I have tried to share some of my personal experiences with God so that maybe others can benefit from them.

It is to be noted that throughout these writings I mention myself often as there seems to be no other way of presenting the blessings God bestows. I encourage all who read this to remember that it is God's grace and generous love that permit me to have these experiences and not anything special in me.

I ask forgiveness if these writings seem full of pride for they are not intended to be and I ask all to thank God if they are touched by this not me for I deserve no thanks.

God love you,

Alan Ames

The Passion of Love

My desire is to totally abandon myself in Christ, to be lost in His love, as my soul can never be satisfied in the things of the world. The hunger I have within cannot be fed with anything else except Christ, Our Lord.

I feel I am wandering in this world, staggering through each day, longing to be only one in God yet, stopped by the distractions of the world from being one in Him. I see my weakness of faith, my self-centeredness, and the worldly desires I hold onto are barriers that separate me from Christ and His glorious love.

In my heart and soul is a continuous longing to feel His love, to experience the fullness of joy that is found within His love. A longing that drives me to search for Our Divine Lord in each moment, in each thought, in each action, in each word, in each sight, in all of my ways and in all of my feelings.

The passion of love I experience when He touches me is the passion of love I want to feel always. When He exposes His love to me and embraces my soul, my spirit, my heart, my physical self, all of me in His love, I know the fullness of love and of life and this fullness I desire to have forever. I never want it to leave me and I am saddened when it does, when I am distracted with thoughts of self and of the world. How I desire the grace to keep my focus totally on Him, knowing if I do so His glorious love will fill my open heart. Knowing too that as my open heart is filled with His love my heart will be opened to others in love so that my love for others can be brought to fullness too. Then in that full love of others, by God's grace, I would find in and through loving others another way to experience the love of Christ, for in each person His love resides even though it may be hidden. With a heart and soul longing to find the love of God in others, this hidden love that all have but so few know about, would be revealed in its glory and in that revelation others could discover the divine gentle love of Christ and come to love Him also.

Yet, as I reflect on this I wonder is it selfish that I should seek such a union of love with Christ, my Lord, when others are much more deserving than I?

This truth eats away at me as I remember how I hurt the One who loves me and there are others who have hurt Him so little. Surely they are more deserving than I. Yet, I know Jesus, my Lord, loves me. I know He has forgiven me and I know He desires I keep seeking to live totally for Him. So as I want to please the One

I love I persist in this seeking of a total abandonment in Him.

I know in doing so that my marriage will be complete, for as I am lost in Him my wife will find herself drawn into His heart. Not because of my desire to abandon self into Him but by the grace He will pour out through this abandonment that will touch the depths of her soul and bring the strong love she has for Him to a crescendo of sacramental love of Our God.

The Doorway

FROM THE MOMENT Jesus, Our Lord, touched and caressed my soul with His love a doorway opened. It was a doorway of love through which the Lord led me. It is through this doorway I discovered, by the grace of God, the Father's love and the Holy Spirit's love. Jesus led me deep into the Trinitarian heart of love that is God's heart. A love so overpowering, a love that is beyond the senses, yet it is felt deep within the soul, a love that sets the soul on fire. A fire I never want to stop burning. A fire which I want to grow and grow so that the flames of love God sets alight within reach out to burn away the evil in the world as it sets fire to the souls of others.

This Trinitarian love, while it is the same love with the Father, as with the Son and the Holy Spirit is different with each. This love is like a fountain of fire flowing within, pouring out ever stronger love, pouring out ever tender love, pouring out ever merciful love. Oh such sweet love that fills the being with the knowledge of the truth that God is One, yet God is Three. That God is love; never ending love for all. That in God all was created, all exists and all can be eternally.

In this divine love comes the understanding that it is only in God's love, full and true love and true life can be found. In this divine love I know God loves me and that God desires my love as He does with every person. I know now that this love is the reason for life and it is the reason for existence. So now I only want to exist in Him, the Father and the Son and the Holy Spirit. I know if I, by God's Grace, can attain this state of total abandonment in Christ, Our Lord, I will also abandon myself in the Father and the Holy Spirit. How I long for this yet I know in myself this is impossible but in God everything is possible and I seek from Him the loving grace to make this possible.

Oasis of Love

IN MY LIFE before I knew God I was walking blindly through a desert. This desert was one I created in my denial of God. I was alone in my selfishness and sinfulness as I distanced myself from God by thinking only of self and distanced myself from others by not caring about them. Every step I took in this desert was a step further away from the reality of God and deeper into the illusion of self. The sand I walked upon was the people I walked over in life as I used and abused them. The ever-hotter sun was the inferno of hell reaching in through my sins to burn my soul. The increasing thirst was the addictions I had drawing my life from me. Yet, in my blindness of pride I was unaware of the barren world I had created and lived in.

It was only when an oasis of love appeared before me, beckoning me to it, that I started to see the truth.

As I changed direction and headed toward the oasis it became clearer and clearer what a world I had created for myself in sin. Then on that glorious day when I reached the oasis of love I was at first hesitant, unsure whether to enter its waters or not. Unsure if the oasis would welcome me or reject me. Tentatively I put my foot into the water not knowing what to expect. As the water touched my skin its coolness comforted my flesh, its gentle touch invited me to enter completely in the waters of love. With great anticipation and excitement I entered up to my waist and as the water engulfed me I felt a love I had never known before. I knew the water loved me. I knew the water wanted to cleanse me and I knew the water would truly wash away the thirst for sin I had.

As the water gently caressed me I turned to look back at the desert I had left behind and sadness came upon me as I saw how foolish I had been. Now I knew the oasis of love had always been there for me, as it is for all people, and that there had been no need for me to be alone thirsting in the desert.

As the water refreshed my being within it I could feel and hear the words: *'Stay with Me forever.'* My heart beat with excitement at the thought of never leaving the water of love that was surrounding and comforting me. Deep in my soul the words exploded forth, 'Yes, I want to stay with You forever.'

As the words left my mouth I felt for the first time true peace knowing this is where I am meant to be. Then in that realization I also understood that it was only myself that had kept me from my true destiny. Once more then the great pride I have reared its ugly head as it allowed evil to call me back to the desert offering all the delights the world can give. However, now I saw these delights would not and could not last and that in the end the desert awaited. Now these delights held nothing for me as they had become valueless. Now I cried in sorrow at how I had been so easily seduced by them before. Now tears of sorrow ran down my face and dripped into the water. My sadness increased as I thought my tears would pollute the water with the stain of my sins.

Yet, the water cried out, 'Your sins can be washed away in Me if only you ask.'

Then the hand of despair came upon me as I thought of how unworthy I was and thought, 'surely my sin is so great I do not deserve to be washed clean'.

Yet, the water called me into it, it called me to come deeper and deeper.

My mind was still lost in thoughts of despair and self-pity but my soul drove me on. Then I was submerged in the water of love and my whole being felt refreshed, renewed, cleansed and pure. As I looked up through the water I could see a fountain flowing into the oasis and filling it. I followed the fountain with my gaze to its source and there was the One who loves me, high upon a cross with His arms open wide. Flowing from His side from His open heart was the source of the water. 'Forgive me, Lord,' I cried as I knew His love and knew He cared for me. The One who loves me raised His head and smiled at me as He said, 'Of course, My friend, of course.' Then I saw there was another fountain flowing from His side, a fountain of blood. 'Come to Me,' the One who loves me called. With uncertainty in myself but not in Him I stepped forth to stand under the fountain of blood.

As the blood washed over me I knew then I loved Him. I knew then this is what I was created to do. I knew then that never again would I stop loving Him and I knew I just wanted to be His. As I looked at the blood washing over me I saw another within it, (a man dressed in black wearing a white collar). He invited me towards him as the One who loves me and the one I love gently encouraged me saying, 'Go.' As I went to the man and fell to my knees all of my wrongs came from my heart and soul and I called from the depth of my being, 'Forgive me.' With a comforting tone the man replied, 'By the grace of the One who loves you, you are forgiven.' As he said these words and raised his hand to make the sign of love I fell backwards into the water. Deeper and deeper I fell but I had no fear for all around me I could feel tenderness, mercy, compassion and love. The deeper I fell the brighter the water became and the stronger the feeling of love grew.

The words, 'Into the depths of My love,' came from the One who loves me.

Now I just wanted to remain there forever, sinking ever deep into the eternal oasis of love. Now my entire being, mind, body, soul and humanity resounded with love. Now no longer did I desire anything except the water of love. Then the One who loves me spoke, saying,

‘Many do not drink of this water and do not know of this water. Go tell them.’ Inside me a desire began to grow, a desire that all should come and bathe in the oasis of love so that they could also find the love, the peace, the joy and the security that I have found. The deeper into the water I went the stronger this desire became because the more you are immersed in the water of love and of life the more you desire to share it.

Discipline of Love

As I SANK into the depths of the Lords' love His love touched the depths of my heart. Now the deepest recesses of my very being could feel His love embracing me. Now within my being was the certainty of God's love and the truth of His love. Now the deceptions, temptations and the falseness of worldly ways became obvious and unwanted. It was now in His love truth washed away the blindness of pride and of self. As the fullness of soul I was experiencing, lifted my being heavenward inside me was a desire never to lose this glorious love of God again. Now the world and its treasures seemed so small and so empty. Now I felt a freedom of heart and soul, a freedom I had never known before, the freedom of love. As the shackles of the world fell from me all I wanted to do was thank God for such a gift. My inner being cried out in love, 'Freely I give myself to You.'

In that moment I also understood that I was now a prisoner of God's love but a willing prisoner. It is when you are imprisoned in His love because you desire only to exist for His love that true freedom is found. In the prison of God's love there is everything you need, everything your heart and soul desires. Everything good, peaceful, soft, tender, gentle, compassionate, forgiving, merciful and joyful. It is a prison that has no restraint except the self imposed restraints of love to stop you sinning and doing wrong. Willingly you embrace the discipline of love that is needed to keep a person from the grasp of evil. I found this discipline to be a joyful discipline that never seems too heavy, never seems too much of a burden and is only seen as a blessing through which the person can show and express their love of the Lord.

The Grain of Sand

IT IS THE love of God that once it touches a heart and soul brings that person to goodness. Once accepted the love of God changes a person either in a little or large way according to what is needed. His Divine love opens up and reveals the truth of God, of life and of existence. God's love removes, if accepted by the person, the fog of confusion, doubt and uncertainty that evil tries to envelop all in. God's love is a refreshing breeze of truth, it is the wind of clarity that blows away the smog of sinfulness. Once that Divine wind cleared my sight I saw for the first time how I truly am.

This true knowledge of self leads me, and all those who desire to cling to the truth, away from sin and closer to God. Now even the smallest sin seems so large and brings me the deepest sadness as I realize that through these small sins there is a rejection of God and

His love. Now my inner self cries out in anguish when I commit the smallest of sins for now it appears like a mountain of sin to me. I feel such deep sorrow as I realize how weak I really am. Now it comes upon the person the awareness that it is only in God's loving grace that the discipline and strength of soul needed can be found. A knowledge of the greatness of God's love, grace and mercy enters the mind, the heart and the soul. With this knowledge the reality of self is acknowledged as I see myself as nothing more than a grain of sand in eternity compared to the greatness of God who is everything and in whom everything exists.

In the smallness of self I came to understand now it is only my sinful pride that brings me to believe that I am more than a grain of sand. Yet in the moment of self-realization comes that touch of God's love which lifts the grain of sand up in His divine hand where He looks upon it in love saying, 'You are more than a grain of sand to Me. You are My child whom I love.' As these words penetrate and fill the being tears from the soul, tears of love and tears of joy gush forth as the entire being revels in these words knowing that they are true and that God really does love me as His child.

Light of Love

As the Lord's love touches and fills my soul the light of His love envelops it.

In this light the soul shines brightly as it is glorified in God's love. Experiencing this divine light, this divine glory brings the certainty of the knowledge of God's loving truth. As I was drawn into His light it became obvious how wrong sin is and how the dark is to be avoided at all costs. In the light of God is all that is good, whereas in the darkness is all that is bad.

In the light, peace and tranquillity surround and fill the soul with the ecstasy of God's love. In the dark it became clear there is only turmoil and confusion that fills the soul with misery.

How grateful to God am I that He, for no other reason than He loves me, lifted me out of the dark and into the light of His love. It was and is in this divine light I long to stay where the sweetness of God's love inebriates my soul with joy. It is here I came to know life outside the light has little true meaning and that living outside the light only leads to eternal darkness and the misery that is within it. The smallest sin now seems so large as it becomes clear that these small sins are stains of darkness that remove me from the light of God. It is as the darkness enters a soul through sin, unless it is rejected immediately, it spreads like a cancer which blocks out the light of God and opens the soul to greater and greater darkness.

As I came to discover this truth a hatred for sin grew within me. Now when I sin at times a sorrow fills my heart as I know then that darkness has pierced my soul. I am driven by the longing to remain in the light of God's love to confess my sins so that once more my soul can be free of darkness. Yet, foolishly,

I repeat my little sins, which in truth are not little, for when you understand what they are they all seem so large. How weak I feel when I realize I have allowed my pride, my impatience and my selfishness to take hold. However, as I confess I feel the precious blood of Jesus washing over me, I see the fountain of forgiving love flowing from His side and I see the Holy Spirit of God bathing my soul in the blood of Christ healing the self inflicted wounds of sin. As the wounds close and the darkness leaves my soul, by God's grace, the light of love returns and my soul sings out joyful thanks to God that He would love me so much.

With my soul shining bright filled with His diving light I am lifted to Him, drawn close to Him and embraced by Him so as to become one in His divine light. In that light the peace and tranquillity return and my heart knows no fear, doubt or uncertainty as now it knows contentment existing in that divine light of love.

Hurt of Heart

As I struggle with self and my weaknesses, trying to remain in the light of love, my heart hurts for the love of God. I know it is the struggle within that causes this pain, for as I struggle with my humanity and all its frailties, the light of the Lord seems to fade. As my attention is taken away from that seeking of grace, of love and of the light of God, and onto self, the pain of heart grows as my heart and soul desire only to seek God. Yet my mind draws me back to self and to my inadequacies.

It is a constant battle to look beyond self and the world. It is a constant struggle with my humanity to keep looking for God. Yet by His divine grace and despite my weak self, God lifts my soul up in His love offering all the strength I need to remain in His love. As I reach out to grasp the strength He offers it seems ever elusive. This strength seems to slip through my fingers as I try to hold onto it. The harder I hold the more it seems to slip by me. As I reach out to the Divine One, I never seem to be able to embrace Him fully as my inner-most-self desires. This is because I still embrace self and cannot seem to let go of self, which is essential if I am to fully embrace the Lord.

It is in this denial of God that the pain of soul and the hurt of heart increase for they can never be truly satisfied and truly at peace until I am totally one in Christ Our Lord. It is in embracing self through self pity, condemnation of self because of one's weaknesses, and despair because one believes God could not love such a person, that so often I seem to let go of God and am trapped in self and so deny God. I deny Him my complete attention, my complete love and my complete acceptance that He does love me. If I cannot accept His total love of me, how can I love Him totally? If I cannot accept His call to come to Him and to be absorbed into Him in a union of love, how can I expect to live completely for Him?

However, even as I reflect on the struggles I have with self I feel the touch of His tender love on my soul, the touch that fills me with the knowledge that despite my faults and failings the Lord just loves me. The touch that fills my soul with joy and soothes the hurt I feel within. The touch that brings my focus back onto the Lord for how could it be anywhere else when this sweetest of loves, this gentlest of loves, this greatest of loves, this love which is divine love caresses my soul and lifts it on high.

Now, looking to the Lord I know He will never let go of me for He loves me. Now, looking to the Lord I know His love never slips by, it just surrounds me. Now, looking to the Lord there is the knowledge that His heart hurts when my heart hurts, for our hearts are one in love.

Now, looking to the Lord it becomes clear these thoughts of self are just a trap set to lead me from the Lord.

However, it is obvious now that the Lord will free me from this trap if I so desire. Now my soul cries out, 'Yes Lord, I desire it, free me.'

My Lord replies, 'In Me you are free, it is only your self that allows you to become a prisoner.'

How foolish I have been for there in the Lord's words is the truth.

I am a prisoner in self and I do not have to be, for in the Lord I can be totally free.

Freedom

My desire is that Jesus will also be free in me to do with me what He will. I do not want to shackle Him by my refusal of giving myself totally to Him. I know my Lord also desires that I give Him the freedom to rule my heart and soul with His tender love so that in His divine will my will becomes one. I realize now that the Lord, if I so let Him, will possess me completely while at the same time set me completely free in His love. Then with His ownership of my soul, my heart, and my life, He will lift me on high to experience the eternal beauty of His divine self.

Understanding this I seek this total freedom that is found when God completely owns me so that the highest levels of grace can be savoured by me, the lowest of the low. As I look to the Lord, my Master, and reach out to Him as a slave of love, I feel Him taking my entire being into His. I feel a drawing of my humanity into His divinity and a lifting of my soul to the highest heights. As the ecstasy of eternal love envelopes me I know that this is the reason for my existence. I am aware now as God reveals His love to me that He created me to live eternally with Him in His glorious, joyful and divine love. How I ache with love, how I hurt with love, and how I am filled with the desire that all should come to know this, the truth of love. No earthly love compares, no earthly love satisfies the soul as God's love does.

With my soul saturated with God's divine love I want only to be with Him forever. I want my soul and every soul to live in this eternal bliss. Now life on earth seems so unimportant yet I know that it is very important for it is through living this earthly life for God that the heavenly life can be found. Now I want to leave the world behind and to live in this state of sanctification forever. Raising my eyes to God I see Him calling me deeper and deeper into His love, calling, 'Come to Me not by yourself, but bring others with you.'

Then inside the deepest recess of my soul is an explosion of grace that I know is the grace God gives to be shared with others so that they can find this heavenly love of God too.

It has become clear by this grace, that to truly be free in God's love I cannot keep His love to myself but must freely share it with others. Now my heart cries out its love for God and cries out its love for others because my heart truly begins to love as God so desires. Now as Jesus, my love and my Lord, reigns supreme in my heart and soul He has the freedom to change my heart as He wills and so He changes it to be one that loves all as He loves all. As this happens my thoughts return to my weak self and immediately I implore the Lord not to let my weaknesses stop me loving. Then the strength of His love washes over me and I know He will keep opening my heart to others even when I close it in the weakness of my pride. I know the Lord will do all that is required to help me love as He wants and all that is required of me is that I keep seeking to do so. Feeling inside me that ecstatic love of God, I know by His grace I will never stop seeking to love as He desires. How could I for I have tasted His sweet love and that in itself drives me on.

Fragrance of Love

For the soul that loves God there is the fragrance of love in every moment. It is not a fragrance that has to be searched for but is experienced in each moment as a normal part of life. It is in living for the love of God and subduing one's will completely to it that a person, by the grace of God, opens their heart and soul to grow in His love and to be able to experience His love in all things at all times. Now as a person lives this way the divine fragrance of love surrounds and fills their every moment. Through this divine love the person then begins to see and feel God's love constantly. God's love permeates all they do so that every action, every thought and every word is filled with love. Their intention now is to experience true love in everything and so they begin to.

As the person looks to others no matter who they are the glory of God's love is seen in the image of God before them that was created by God's love. As a person looks to the world around, it now becomes a kaleidoscope of love showing different aspects of God's divine love in even what may seem so insignificant to others. Now nothing is seen as valueless as everything is appreciated for the love in which it was given and the love in which it exists.

As the air fills the lungs so does the sweet taste of God's love. Now each intake of air is like inhaling God's breath and as this divine breath fills the being, the joy of knowing that even in this God is filling the person with His generous love explodes within.

In this state of love the person now becomes what God wants them to be; a beacon of love in a world filled with sin, immorality and selfishness. A beacon that shines brightly with love dispersing the dark, leading others out of despair and into the loving hope of God. To others now the person becomes a fragrance of love, for as God's love fills their every moment His divine love united in human love emits sweet tender love to all. It is in this state the person becomes Christ to the world as the merciful and forgiving love of Jesus is magnified through them and is poured out through them to fill the lives of others with the eternal fragrance of love.

Perfection

EACH DAY THERE is a battle between my spirit, which desires only to achieve perfection in Christ and my body and mind which, in their weakness, draw me to sin. My mind takes my focus onto self and my body desires satisfaction in the world. Yet my spirit cries out to God in love. My spirit is drawn to God in love. My spirit only wants what is of God to fill it. Unlike my mind and body which seem to want what is of the world. I wonder how it is that the weaknesses of my mind and body can at times be stronger than my spirit. I wonder how, with such flaws in my being, I can reach the wonderful state of perfection my spirit and my soul desire and long for. Then I realize that it is through this daily battle I am being led by God to perfection. I see and feel how He pours out grace in each struggle to give me the strength I need to overcome the weaknesses I have. I see that it is by embracing this grace and facing each weakness with it that I am being purified of my weaknesses and take small but definite steps towards the perfection my inner self desires.

It becomes obvious too that in the Sacraments of the Eucharist and Reconciliation my spirit is enriched as my soul is fed and purified by the presence, love and grace of God. I come to understand that the state of perfection I long for can be experienced in the Sacraments if I will be completely open to God in them. Then with a little sadness it becomes clear that to live in this perfect state is only possible after death when God in His love would permit me to reside in heaven with Him. There also comes the realization that to reach heaven I must continue to seek perfection on earth even though I cannot in self achieve this as a permanent state because it is by seeking and struggling to reach perfection on earth that the perfect state of eternal life in heaven is found.

In the love of Christ I am wounded by my weaknesses as each one of them hurts me deeply. The knowledge that each of my weaknesses is a holding onto self and not a complete embracing of Christ hurts me more than physical pain. My heart and soul cry out in agony as I deny them complete immersion in Christ, Our Lord's love, the sweet love that satisfies the soul fully. The divine love that brings the human heart to the highest of heights, the glorious love that brings the being into the true glory of Christ's love. Deep inside my self cries out, 'Do not deny me this love.' Deep inside, deep in the recesses of my soul, my spirit yearns for the fire of

God's love, the fire that illuminates, the fire that burns away the darkness. The fire that warms me with the tender caresses of Christ Himself. Oh my God I want this so much yet through my weaknesses I keep denying myself Your love. No wonder the wounds caused by my weaknesses hurt so much, for I see they are self inflicted wounds through which I deny myself what I truly desire and I truly need; the perfect love of Christ.

Sweet Joy

WHEN THE SWEET joy that is Jesus' love touches my heart and soul my being experiences what awaits in heaven. This knowledge of heavenly bliss brings me to desire it eternally. This knowledge drives me in love to live the way that opens me to the glory of God's love. My soul within me cries out for this joy to remain within me always. My spirit leads me to seek the heavenly joy in every moment of life in all I do. The grace of God empowers me because of this as my entire being now focused on the joyful love of God is opened to the divine grace God wants to bestow on me and wants to bestow on all people.

This grace, as it strengthens me in my seeking to live for God, also increases the desire for the joy of God's love while at the same time increasing the joy within my heart and soul. So that as the joy increases so does the desire for it. At times it feels as if I am totally submerged in the divine joyful love of God. I feel as if I am lost to the worldly existence while finding the heavenly existence. As I drown in this never ending sea of joy there is no fear of being lost forever, as this is what I now desire. I know that being lost in God's love is where I will truly find myself by the grace of God. I know that it is when I am outside of the divine love that I am lost.

As the warmth of the tender love of God surrounds and embraces me it lifts me beyond the physical joy to an ecstatic state of the soul which no words can describe. As God lifts me up and draws me deep into His loving heart the Lord Jesus shows me there is a place in His heart for each person. He gives me the understanding that in Him there is the same joy for everyone, the same joy I experience. The joy that will not lessen because it is shared but only increases in each person the more it is shared. Now it becomes clear that if God's joyful love is shared amongst and embraced by mankind that through mankind it will be magnified in the physical realm. Then through this magnification of God's love mankind will be raised to experience the spiritual and mystical joy of His divine and eternal love. What a blessing God bestows upon mankind, a blessing I love all to share, a blessing my soul longs to experience constantly and longs for all other souls to experience. A blessing of love.

The Power of Love

FROM THE MOMENT God's love touched my heart and soul it is the power of His love that drives me on and on to seek more of His love. This Divine power elevates my mind beyond the world to thoughts of heaven and what awaits me there. Every day has become a day seeking to love God more, a day seeking to love God in each moment. The times when the sweet Saviour touches me gently with His love, when He tenderly embraces me in His divine self my very being explodes in glorious ecstasy as my soul bathes in the divine heart of love. In these moments my whole being cries its love for the Lord of Love.

As I am immersed in the Almighty God I feel that I am returning to where I was created in love. I feel I never want to leave this place of divine love, divine peace, divine joy and divine mercy. This place which I know is my home. My soul at peace rests contentedly absorbing the loving joy that God offers to me and to all in His divine mercy. With my soul at peace my mind and my body are filled with serenity as my whole being is united in God's love. The physical world around me seems to melt away as the heavenly glory of God envelops me completely. Now I desire to stay like this forever never to return to the world again.

However, the world does not want to let go of me, it holds firmly onto me and draws me back into thoughts of self and of the world. Once more I am imprisoned by my weaknesses as my attention is taken away from God. Oh, why am I so weak that I let this happen? Disappointment with myself fills me as I realize how easily I am distracted from God. Yet, in these moments of self pity my sweet love Jesus reaches out and holds me in His arms. Encouraging me to persevere, encouraging me to keep offering my weaknesses to Him in love so that in the recognition of how fragile I truly am I can once more be open to the power of His love.

Sometimes I feel like I am walking on a tightrope as I try to walk to heaven. Any moment I can slip, any moment I can fall to my destruction. But then the Lord shows me He is there to steady me and to stop me falling. He is there to keep me balanced. So why should I fear? If I hold onto Him nothing can pull me from the tightrope. If I hold firmly to His love the tightrope becomes a wide path which is safe and secure and from which I will never stray. Why does God love me so much that He would put such effort into saving me and helping me? Why does God love all people so much? It is beyond my understanding but deep in my soul I know He does and I know He will never stop loving mankind. My God how can I ever thank You? My God how can I ever repay Your loving kindness? My God whatever it is Lord I give to You please accept my offering and take of me what You will.

Books available from:

USA

Alan Ames Ministry
PO Box 200
233 Glasgow Avenue SW
Kellogg
Minnesota 55945

Phone: 507 767 3027
Web: http://www.alanames.org

Australia

Touch of Heaven
(Alan Ames Ministry)
PO Box 85
Wembley, 6014
West Australia

Phone: 61 89275 6608
Fax: 61 89382 4392
Web: http://www.alanames.ws
Email: touchofheaven@iinet.net.au